# LIVING Between HOPE and Heartache

JESSIE COPELAND

LUCIDBOOKS

**Living Between Hope and Heartache**

Copyright © 2025 by Jessie Copeland

Published by Lucid Books Houston, TX
www.Lucidbooks.com

All rights reserved. No part of this publication may be reproduced, stored in a retrieval system, or transmitted in any form by any means, electronic, mechanical, photocopy, recording, or otherwise, without the prior permission of the publisher, except as provided for by USA copyright law.

Unless otherwise indicated, scripture quotations are taken from the NKJV New King James Version®. Copyright © 1982 by Thomas Nelson. Used by permission. All rights reserved.

ISBN: 978-1-63296-760-2
eISBN: 978-1-63296-761-9

Special Sales: Most Lucid Books titles are available in special quantity discounts. Custom imprinting or excerpting can also be done to fit special needs. Contact Lucid books at info@lucidbooks.com

> For the sake of privacy, some names and personal details have been altered in this memoir.

*First off, this book would not exist without God. All glory is His. If I did not have faith, this story would be very different, and I would not have shared it. Honestly, I don't know where I would be without God and His grace.*

*To my family: You are all such a blessing to me. I thank you for every moment we have spent together—the good moments and the bad. Even in the bad times, we learned something. I love you all so very much; the more we grow, the more your love fills my heart. Truly, my cup runs over.*

*To my teacher friends: Thank you for carrying me through the hard times. Thank you for listening to me. Thank you for advice and opinions. Thank you most of all for the laughter; life without laughter is just no fun! You guys are the best.*

*Thank you to the people around us for caring. I am so very blessed.*

# Table of Contents

| | |
|---|---|
| Preface | vii |
| December 17, 1999 | 1 |
| October 25, 2015 | 3 |
| October 26, 2015 | 9 |
| November 8, 2015 | 15 |
| November 26, 2015 | 17 |
| December 17, 2015 | 21 |
| December 27, 2015 | 23 |
| New Year's Day 2016 | 25 |
| February 28, 2016 | 27 |
| March 27, 2016 | 31 |
| April 23, 2016 | 33 |
| May 13, 2016 | 35 |
| June 9, 2016 | 39 |
| June 11, 2016 | 43 |
| July 6, 2016 | 47 |
| July 7, 2016 | 51 |
| August 8, 2016 | 53 |
| August 18, 2016 | 55 |
| Later That Same Day | 57 |

| | |
|---|---|
| September 9, 2016 | 61 |
| September 10, 2016 | 63 |
| September 30, 2016 | 65 |
| October 10, 2016 | 67 |
| November 13, 2016 | 69 |
| November 14, 2016 | 71 |
| November 15, 2016 | 73 |
| November 18, 2016 | 75 |
| November 19, 2016 | 79 |
| November 21, 2016 | 81 |
| November 25, 2016 | 83 |
| December 17, 2016 | 85 |
| December 21, 2016 | 87 |
| December 23, 2016 | 89 |
| December 25, 2016 | 91 |
| December 30, 2016 | 95 |
| January 8, 2017 | 97 |
| January 22, 2017 | 101 |
| February 11, 2017 | 103 |
| February 20, 2017 | 105 |
| February 22, 2017 | 107 |
| March 20, 2017 | 109 |
| January 17, 2019 | 111 |

# Preface

Millions of families lose loved ones to addiction every day. I'm not just talking about the ones that have to bury their loved ones. If you have ever loved an addict, you know that drugs steal that person away . . . minute by minute. The addiction changes their personality; it slowly changes their bodies physically. You watch as the person you love—your mom, your daughter, your son, your sister, or brother—becomes a stranger. You watch as the love you have begins to shatter.

This story is mine as a mother who watched her daughter fight the battle of addiction. My story ends in a happy place. So many do not.

If you are living your own version of this nightmare, I pray that this story offers you hope. If you are young, I pray that as you read this, you learn from my daughter's mistake. She tried drugs one time—just one time—and her life was stolen for two years. Scars were made that will last a lifetime.

Whatever your circumstance, I pray this story touches your heart.

# December 17, 1999

Oh my sweet baby girl,

Lilly Ann Couper, welcome to this life. Today you were born. Today I finally held you in my arms and saw those beautiful blue eyes—the same eyes I see looking back at me in the mirror. They are the same blue as my mother's eyes.

You are mine. You are perfect. Your dad melted the second he saw you. He snuggled you, and pride shone from his face. It was beautiful. Your brother was swept away by you. He held you in his little two-year-old arms and fell in love. "My baby," he said to you.

I pray we are the parents you deserve. I pray we always do what is best for you in this life. I pray we lead you toward God and teach you His ways. You are an amazing blessing. I just keep kissing your head and breathing you in. My daughter. My sweet girl. I pray I am better at this than my mother. I pray I do not make her mistakes. I promise I will not fail you. I promise to never leave you. I promise to always be here.

Always . . . I love you,
Mama

> *"For this child I prayed, and the Lord has granted me my petition which I asked of Him."*
>
> —1 Samuel 1:27

# October 25, 2015

Where the hell **are** you?

I woke up early this morning after sleeping only a couple of hours. I had a feeling you were going to sneak out . . . again. I was exhausted. I just saw you at four thirty when I got up to check on you because I heard a noise. You were up walking around in your room. I asked why you were up, and you said, "Mom, I got my period. I just got up to change panties!" And like a fool I believed you. I thought, "Well it's already too late; she won't go out. She will go to sleep." Stupid!

I texted at eight o'clock, "Do you want to go to Roswell with me later?" I knew you were high. I knew you weren't sleeping. After ten minutes with no answer and hearing a voice repeating in my head, *Go check on her,* I did . . . you weren't there. I yelled to your dad, "She's gone again."

And then I saw your phone on the floor. My heart stopped. I hit the floor. I may have screamed. Your brother, Tanner, came running. I knew this was more than sneaking out. You're a teenager. You always have your phone. This was it. You had run away. I don't think my brain worked the rest of the day.

We called the police. You sent me a message on Facebook that gave me the password to your phone. You left us a letter. I read it in total shock and disbelief. Man, you put a lot of thought and planning into leaving your family. The policeman said, "She sure does sound confident."

I thought, *Yeah meth does that to her.* I don't know why I didn't say it out loud. I think I was afraid they wouldn't look for you if they knew you had a problem with meth. I didn't know . . . didn't know how bad it was until now. Not until you picked drugs over your family. I am thrown back to memories of my mother. She always picked the drugs . . . or the man who gave her the drugs, over us—my brother and me. It hurts so much more coming from my daughter.

My friends, Faith, and Victoria, came over and went through your phone. Your dad and Tanner went to Artesia and drove around everywhere looking for you. I was useless. I sat under a blanket and stared out the window. My body was freezing, despite the warmth of the house. I kept shivering all day. I think my body wanted to quit. I just kept seeing you . . . dead. I kept imagining your body slumped over on a couch, in a bed, or in a car . . . wherever my brain pictured your lifeless body for a moment. I continued praying that whomever you were with would at least call an ambulance or take you to the hospital if you did overdose.

I had a prayer on repeat in my head . . . so short and basic: "Please God, Please God, Please God, Please God, Please God," over and over. Surely, He knows. He knows I am begging for you—for your safety, your health, your heart. . . . Please God.

## October 25, 2015

It's the same prayer I said in my dreams the night you stayed in Carlsbad at Emily's house when you were thirteen. I told you about it when you got home from Carlsbad. I had a horrible nightmare that you were missing. I can't remember anything except the terror I felt with every fiber of my body. When I woke up from that nightmare, at one in the morning, I sent Emily a text telling her that I knew I was crazy, but to text me in the morning when she woke up and tell me that you were safe. She called me back right away.

She said she woke up with a terrible feeling and ran upstairs to check on you and Jamie. We still believe someone was in the house that night. I believe that God intervened then . . . I know he will again now.

Victoria and Faith gave me a list of contacts they found in your phone. We called and spoke with all of them. So many strangers. All of them knew you. All of them claimed to have no idea where you were. I didn't know any of them. How do you know these people? Do I know anything about you anymore? I just feel like a failure. How did things get so far beyond my control? I really thought I knew you. I thought I knew your friends and what was going on in your life. I now realize that I knew nothing. I thought back over the past year or so. How many times have you lied to me? I go over every story that didn't make sense. I think of your random fainting spells that the doctors couldn't explain. They even did drug tests at the hospital, and nothing turned up. I remember wondering why you looked surprised when the doctor said that. You laughed and said I was crazy—that I was seeing things. Oh my gosh how many times have you told me that this year? "Mom, you're crazy. I didn't say that" . . . or "I didn't do that!" I really thought I was losing my mind.

I kept making excuses for your strange behavior. I kept thinking I was having memory issues. I never ever thought it was drugs. Until you told your dad. I'm not sure why you did that. You had fainted again at the Family Dollar Store. We had already been to the hospital for two other spells and some strange rash that appeared. No answers from anyone. You wouldn't allow the workers at the Dollar Store to call the ambulance, so you called your dad. After he picked you up, you told him you were using meth and begged him not to tell me.

When he said those words, I felt the world stop. Not you. Not **my** daughter. I had always told you how dangerous drugs were. I told you how my mom chose drugs over her children. I told you the damage it caused my brother and me. I took you to meet my family that was so wrapped up in drug abuse and alcohol that they lived in garbage. I showed you the horrors I grew up in! How? How could you choose this? How?

I am writing this letter to you because I am wide awake. How do I sleep when I don't know where you are . . . who you are with . . . what you are doing? I am living my worst nightmare. I want to sleep and wake up when it's over. My heart is shattered. But it's still together thanks to my faith in God, but it's full of cracks—held together by tiny threads. I am not sure how people without faith get through life. How do parents live like this for years and years not knowing where their child is? What if we become those parents?

OCTOBER 25, 2015

How do I do that? I don't think I can. . . . Please God . . . Please God . . . Please . . .

I pray you are home soon. I guess I will see if I can find something to help me sleep. I hope you know I love you wherever you are. I hope you are alive. I hope . . .

I love you so much,
Mom

> *"When I am afraid, I will trust in you."*
> —Psalm 56:3

# October 26, 2015

I couldn't go to work today. I finally took a sleeping pill last night, after staring at the ceiling for hours playing out your death over and over in my head. Today, I feel like a zombie. I don't know how to do this. How do I keep going when I feel so lost? I keep praying, but my prayers at this point don't even have words. Do you think God understands my groans and my tears, my wordless pleas for your life?

Dad and I decided to go to Artesia. Your brother has been everywhere . . . called everyone. I think Dad just wanted to get me out of the house. He keeps staring at me like he's waiting for me to break. I will admit I am close . . . but not there yet. I can get through this until we get the knock on the door. The knock from the Sheriff or the State Police . . . whomever they send to break the news to us. The news that the drugs won . . . that they stole you away. Then I will break. I just hope I can put myself back together. I hope . . .

I remembered something you said about a boy . . . what was his name, Gael? Anyway, you said he lived over by Steven's grandma, so we drove back that way. I spoke to Gael on the phone yesterday . . . and to his mom. They both said they had heard from you and that you said you were OK. They said you went with a friend to get away from here. Something didn't fit in their stories. I am positive you're there . . . or at least, they know where you are.

We drove down a road and saw several crappy abandoned houses—some trailers falling apart . . . no doors or windows. One didn't even have a roof. I just kept staring and wondering if you were hiding in one of those nasty places. Then I saw a purple trailer. I remember one of your friends, Hannah, said something about seeing your car at a purple trailer a few weeks back. I told Dad this was it. We stopped. I got out and knocked on the door. Some lady answered. She was wearing a negligee. Then the smell hit me—something like a mix of mildew, trash, and cat urine. It was awful. There was a leak right in front of the door. Water was pouring into a bucket while "Negligee Lady" was staring at me. *Why is there water?* I thought; *it isn't raining.* I feel like I am living in slow motion. Negligee Lady clears her throat.

Oh. Yeah. "Hi . . . I am Lilly's mom. Is Gael here?"

"Oh yes, but he is asleep," she replies. I notice two children behind her. Two sweet-faced, filthy little children. Sitting on the couch giggling and whispering. I hear one say your name.

"Can I please come in and talk to him. I just want to find my daughter." My voice cracks, and the tears well up.

"OK," she says.

I walk into the death trap these people call home. I hold my breath and walk through the kitchen and down the hall. There he is. The boy I spoke to over the phone—the one who said you called him and said you were OK. He is lying on a mattress on the floor. The floor is covered in laundry. It breaks my heart that

## October 26, 2015

you would call this twit and not your family . . . anger sits on the top of my tongue. I ask him if he has heard from you. He won't look at me. He threw his arm over his eyes. He mumbles something about you haven't called since we spoke yesterday. He won't look at me. My anger was building.

His mom, Negligee Lady, is standing next to me in the hallway. She laughs and pushes someone into the bathroom. "My husband," she says.

I didn't ask. I don't care. I hate these people. My anger is boiling because inside I know they know where you are. I crack. I scream, " I just want my daughter back!"

I turn and walk out. Negligee Lady keeps trying to hug me. She is so high. I don't even think she remembers why I am there. The little kids just stare. I am probably scaring the crap out of them. I walk out of the house. Back to your dad. Away from this hell that reminds me of my childhood. I can't believe you would choose these people. Is this where you are? Is this what you want to do with your life? Can the high possibly be that great?

I see the Artesia School resource officer walking up to the door of the death trap. We exchange glances. I get in the pickup and tell your dad how gross the house was . . . how they are all lying. And then I cry . . . again. I bet he is tired of seeing me cry. He is sweet. He rubs my back.

"Let's go to the Sheriff's office and see if they can tell us anything," he says. I nod. We drive away from the death trap and stop up the road at Steven's. I knock on his door. He comes out, and we talk for a minute—this boy that you loved just last year. Your first real boyfriend. He knows nothing, he says. He will call if he hears anything. He looks worried and kind of sad. He won't really look at me. No one will. I am so tired of having this conversation already. I just want you home.

The Sheriff's office is empty. No help again. We are driving home. I feel hopeless and deflated.

Tanner calls. "I am going to pick her up. She called me. Mom, I'm going now." And just like that, I can breathe again. A weight lifts off my soul. You're alive. You are coming home. Thank you, Jesus . . . Thank you.

Twenty minutes later, you walked through the door, and I hugged you. You smelled like the death trap. I want to scream at you. I want to slap your face. You just push me away and go to your room. You lie down like you're exhausted. I can't talk to you. Who is this girl who has stolen my daughter?

So, I write this letter. I don't even know why. You don't seem to care at all. You don't care that my heart is shattered or that your brother was frantic looking for his baby sister. You don't care when the Sheriff comes and is questioning you. You just throw an attitude at all of us. So much so that the Sheriff's deputy tells your dad he is allowed to swat you. You act like this is not a big deal at all. Eventually, the Sheriff leaves. I want to talk to you, but your dad tells me to give you some space. He says to let you rest.

OCTOBER 26, 2015

I am so lost. How can I fix this? All I see is the addiction. I see years with my mother and the situation never improving. I am going to find a way to help you. I cannot let you fall like my mother did. So I end this letter with a promise. I will find a way to help you beat this. That's my job, right? I am your mom. I will fix it.

# November 8, 2015

Dear Lilly,

I am still writing letters because you won't talk to me. Not about anything important anyway. You started counseling this week. You were angry when you saw your counselor. She used to be a teacher at your middle school. Science. I am not sure why she is a counselor now. She probably got sick of the direction education is heading. I am a teacher. I understand. Anyway, at first you were angry, but after your first session you seemed OK. You said she was nice and gave you a lot of information that was helpful. I guess she asked you to journal about everything. I was happy because I believe you will do better if you feel a connection with your counselor. I just want you to have your life back. I want to have my daughter back.

You're angry because we moved you back to school in Hagerman. You had been excited to go to a new school. You have been here in Hagerman since kindergarten—same school, same teachers, same friends. Your brother moved to Artesia in his junior year and loved it. You wanted to try it. Something new. You wanted away from this small town and everyone who knows all your business. We tried. It hasn't even been a semester. You're not you anymore, so we made you come back. I work right next door, so we are hoping to keep a closer eye on you.

It has only been a couple of weeks since you ran away. I know you're irritated because I seem to be next to you at every moment. I know because I am even annoying myself. I just can't seem to let you out of my sight. I am trying to quit being crazy. I am. It's so hard. When you're not with me, I am almost in a panicked state of mind. Can I get post-traumatic stress from this situation? I feel like I can. I feel so worried all the time. I am barely sleeping. I get up ten times a night to check that you are still here—still in your room. It's exhausting. My entire life is suffering. I am a walking zombie all day every day. I don't know how I am working. I don't know what I am teaching these poor first graders. I am constantly checking in on my phone to see where you are. My brain is worried about you every moment.

I have hope. I notice small changes. You're coming out of your room more. You even smile every now and then. The counselor suggested an over-the-counter vitamin that is supposed to help with depression. She says that depression is a severe side effect of quitting meth. I keep researching stories online about meth abuse. I have hope. Maybe soon I will give you these letters, and we will talk about how much better your life is now. Maybe.

I love you more. More than your addiction. More than the anger. More than anything that has happened.

Always,
Mom

# November 26, 2015

Dear Lilly,

Today is Thanksgiving. We drove to my sister's house in Odessa. I was looking forward to this day because my brother Jeff was going to be there. I have never met him. We started talking on the phone and writing letters when I was about eighteen. He was sixteen. That's when I found out that he existed, and we have kept in touch ever since. I am now thirty-eight. I wanted to be more excited about meeting him, but my focus was elsewhere.

I spent the entire day trying to decide if your pupils were dilated. Were you too hyper? Too quiet? Did you go anywhere alone? I am driving myself crazy and everyone else too. I know you tell your counselor I am insane. Maybe I am. I don't know how to keep going and act like life is "normal." I am constantly afraid you're going to use again. My brain is always thinking, *What can I do to stop her? How can I keep my baby girl safe?* I know these are crazy thoughts. Somewhere in my rational mind, I know I am losing my mind, but I can't stop.

I miss the days when you were little. I miss being able to kiss your boo-boos away. Your brother feels like I am ignoring him completely . . . I probably am, and I don't even realize it. I feel like I am trying to maintain some kind of normalcy. I thought I was doing well. Your dad took me out driving around the other day just to get out of the house. It was probably more to give you space, since I won't leave you alone for a moment. Dad kept watching me as we drove. He talked about this and that. I don't even remember what he said to be honest. Finally, he says, "Well, I guess I will never be able to make you happy." I heard that. I heard that down to the core of my being. I was hurting him. I am hurting him and my son and you. I have to dig myself out of this dark pit I have fallen into. I am so sad because you walked right into the life that I fought so hard to get out of.

My mother started smoking pot after her dad died when she was about thirteen. She stayed high or drunk most of her teenage years. My grandma, a young widow with five children, stayed drunk after the death of my grandpa, so she didn't really notice what my mom was up to. My mom ended up pregnant with me when she was sixteen. Two years later, she had my brother. My dad split soon after. I don't know for sure what happened next. I remember Don Bishop. I remember him beating the crap out of my mom on a regular basis. I remember his late-night visits to my bedroom. I remember finding my mom passed out with a needle in her arm. I went to her room because I found a tick on my leg. I thought it was going to drink all my blood and that I would die. I was five or six. She kept shooting whatever was in that needle up her arm. She passed out on the bed, and I sat on the floor and cried thinking I was going to die.

My grandma took us in when I was in fourth grade. I am not sure why. I blocked a lot of things out. She was still drinking but kept it hidden well. She was much more stable . . . well a little more stable than my mom. I was screwed up. I needed

## November 26, 2015

help, but no one really noticed. I didn't realize it then, but God kept me going. I never turned to drugs or drinking. My fear of turning into my mother was stronger than the need to get rid of any painful memories. Plus, I became very good at forgetting. At the age of fourteen, I moved in with my dad. I had met him once before, along with his wife and his four daughters. I barely knew them, and I am sure they didn't want a seriously screwed up, angry teenage girl, but I knew I had to get away from my family. My uncles were all heavy drug users, and my brother was becoming one.

My mom still popped up occasionally and drove me crazy. I had to get out . . . and now here I am so many years later facing this situation all over again. But this time, I have to find a way to save you. My mom couldn't be saved. Right before you were born, she was killed in Las Vegas. She was hit by an SUV on the Las Vegas strip as she was running away from an angry boyfriend. She wasn't high; she was five times over the legal limit for alcohol. I have to find a way to save you and save myself.

Please, God, please. I cannot do this without you. I love you, baby girl.

# December 17, 2015

Today you turn sixteen. I can't believe it. In some ways, it seems as if you were born just the other day. So small and sweet. You were stubborn before birth. You were due on December 9, but you had no desire to get out of my belly. Well, not until the doctor decided to induce. Then you decided to come three hours before they started the medicine to begin the labor. I should have known from the beginning you would not be easy.

Life has been a little better since my last letter. You seem to have mellowed out some, and so have I. I discovered roller derby, and I am excited. God sent this my way right after my last letter. I needed a way out of my pit, and roller derby has been a dream of mine since I was a kid. I have backed off my intense focus on you. I am just trying to do my own thing. Your brother is busy with work. He seems happier too. Maybe life is getting back to normal. We didn't have a party to celebrate your birthday; instead, we had a nice dinner and some cake. You seemed like yourself. I love you so much. I just enjoyed watching you laugh and enjoy the day. These moments are so rare. I am usually the one screwing them up. The other day we went shopping, and the day was so nice.

We stopped by Hastings so I could look for a book, and we got some coffee. You got really excited about some magazine with pictures of Marilyn Monroe. I guess I gave you my "Are you high?" look. You noticed right away, and all the excitement left your body like air leaving a balloon. I saw the tears build up in your eyes. I couldn't take it back. When I apologize, you just deflate more. I am really getting good at making this worse. Today though, for your birthday, I didn't have the look. I didn't say anything stupid. I just sat back and enjoyed your laugh. Sixteen years. They flew by. I pray this next year will be much happier than the last. I pray this is you becoming you again and that the drugs are quickly becoming a memory we can forget about. Oh, Lord, I pray.

I love you.
Mom

# December 27, 2015

Dear Lilly,

So Christmas has come and gone. It was good. We didn't do much, but we had a good time. The craziest thing happened this morning though. Yesterday on the news the weatherman said we were under a blizzard warning . . . us! A blizzard! Don't they know this is the desert? That's the craziest thing ever . . . or so I thought. I literally laughed at the weatherman.

By five in the afternoon, we had some low clouds. That was it. By seven, it was snowing. By nine, we couldn't see across the driveway; the snow was coming down and blowing so hard. I have never seen anything like it. When I woke up this morning, I could not believe my eyes. There were six-foot snowdrifts! There had to be at least a foot on the ground. I mean this is Hagerman, New Mexico! We don't get snow like this. Watching your face when you woke up was great. You were so excited, like a little kid. It made my heart happy to see. We spent the day watching movies and just hanging out. You went outside and played with your dog, Katniss, in the yard for a bit. She loved the snow, and you loved watching her. Watching you have fun and be "normal" makes me feel like a huge weight has been lifted off me. There are moments like this every now and then—moments when I am not scared to death that I am going to lose you. The best part was that I know there is no way for you to leave.

No way to sneak out. You're stuck here. Wow, that sounds really mean. You have been so much better . . . I am probably not being fair. I am just really looking forward to going to bed tonight and being able to sleep. Not listening for every sound . . . not getting up to check if you're still in bed. Your dad drilled huge pieces of tin over your window after you ran away, so you haven't really tried to get out.

I can't turn it off though, that fear that you will slip away undetected. Maybe tonight. Maybe I can sleep since you can't sneak out in a foot of snow. The roads are completely impassable, so no one can pick you up and help you escape. I just want to sleep and not worry that you won't be here when I wake up. I wish this sounded more like love and less like insanity. I keep praying about my psychotic behavior, but it doesn't seem to get any better. I swear it is coming from a place of love; it just looks like a crazy, overprotective, control freak mom. So not the person I wanted to be.

Drugs change everything. I love you.
Mom

# New Year's Day 2016

Dear Lilly,

I can't believe we made it through another year. This one was hard. You and I are talking a little more every day. You seem to be more and more yourself most of the time, but there are still moments when I wonder. I am finally starting to sleep a little better. At least now I am getting a few hours at a time. It helps me function better. You laugh more than you have in a while. You and Tanner seem really close lately, and that makes my soul smile. Every mother loves to see her children getting along. I always pray if anything ever happens to me that you will lean on each other. I love you both so much—so much more than I ever knew was possible. I didn't grow up with relationships like that.

My mom popped in and out after my grandma took us away. She and I did not get along at all. She always tried to act like she was still eighteen, and she would wear my clothes, which of course I hated. I remember getting into a huge fight with her, because I told her she was fat and would stretch out my clothes. She slapped me, and I lost it. I went after her with full force. My grandma broke us up and yelled at me. I was so mad. Everyone was so scared to make my mom mad. They were afraid she would leave again. I knew she was planning to leave before she even got there. She never planned to stay. Sure enough, two days later, she stole my grandma's new VCR and was gone for another year or so. They all blamed me. I was never really close with anyone—not even my brother. Not really.

Now though, I look at you and your brother and I just can't imagine how I lived without that kind of love before. You both mean everything to me. I wish I could let you feel how much I want you to have a good and happy life. I don't even have words to describe how it hurts me to see you struggling with this. I mean, yes things now are much better. You're home. You're not sneaking out (as far as I know). You really seem to be trying. You are making progress. But I see the struggle in your eyes. I know you're still wanting to get high. You're wanting to give in and feel good. I hate it. I would take it away from you in a heartbeat. I would feel every ounce of misery for you, if I could. The hardest thing I have ever done in my life is watch your life fall apart and know that I cannot do anything at all to help. I pray every night that God will take care of this for you. I think he will. Why would he allow me to go through this again? I pray. I go to church every once in a while. I read my Bible sometimes. I know I am not perfect, but I try hard to do the right thing.

Maybe I should try harder. Maybe my failures as a mother are why you are facing this hard time. I don't know. I know I love you more than words can explain. I know I will always be here. I know that God has a plan and that someday, we will all be OK. I hope we will all be happy. Whatever comes, we will get through it.

Love you, baby girl,
Mom

# February 28, 2016

Dear Lilly,

Today is your dad's birthday. We didn't really plan much. Just made a cake—German chocolate— his favorite. It feels like everyone in this house lives in a different world. This month has been rough. As we sat around and ate the cake, hardly any words were spoken. This sucks.

I broke my ankle earlier in the month. I would love to be able to say I broke it during a derby bout and that some tough chick hit me and snap I went down. That would sound cool. No. I broke it wearing skates. On grass. Like an idiot. I stepped off the concrete—literally one step. I didn't use the stopper and snap. I hit the ground. My friend's husband carried me to my car. My friend drove me home. Dad looked at me like I was being a big baby. We called the local EMT, and he checked it out. He said it didn't look broken. I sat at home for two days. I tried to put weight on it. I used a crutch to get around. My foot started turning black. I was pretty sure that wasn't normal, so you drove me to the ER. Yeah, my ankle was broken. I felt ridiculous.

I learned that I am not good at asking for help or accepting help, for that matter. My friend offered me a scooter to use at school, and I threw a fit like a four-year-old. You are driving me everywhere and carrying all my junk since I am on crutches.

You are just pissed off all the time. You don't complain; you just roll your eyes a lot. I was hoping that having you help me would help us grow closer. I think maybe it has done the opposite. I had to have surgery on my ankle a few days ago. Tanner drove me to the surgery and back home. I have been pretty occupied with my own stuff, so I haven't had time to follow you around and accuse you of breathing wrong. Maybe that's a good thing. I don't know. I am a firm believer that everything happens for a reason. I guess roller derby isn't in the cards at the moment.

I hate the silence around this house. I hate that I can't fix it even more. I just sat and watched everyone eat cake and stare at their phones. Your dad made eye contact with me for a moment. Even my relationship with him is strained. He says I am too hard on you. I jump to conclusions too easily. I know he is right. I hate the way my brain is constantly looking for signs to see if you're high. I can't turn it off. I pray all the time that God would show me if something is happening so that I will quit worrying the rest of the time. That prayer isn't working. My worry is constant. Even when I'm busy with other stuff. Even while I was lying there waiting to go into surgery. I wondered where you were, what you were doing—wondered if I had done everything I could to make sure I would know if you ditched school? Oh how I wish I could turn it off.

I am losing it. I know that if I can't quit, I am going to push you away. I feel how much you hate me all the time. It's awful. When I try to hug you, your whole body gets tense, like I disgust you. It breaks my heart. How strange to be the hated mother.

## February 28, 2016

Is this how my mom felt? I remember hating her hugs. I would cringe at the sound of her voice. I had so much anger when she would show up. I am sure she could see it. I see it in you. Wow . . . I have become the hated parent. Not because I left, but because I keep pushing. Oh, how I don't want to ruin this relationship. I love you. I guess my mother loved me. Funny how my relationship with you is teaching me things about the mother I didn't really know. Oh well, I guess this letter isn't saying much. I just wish we could talk. I miss my daughter.

# March 27, 2016

So, this morning your friend Katie's family invited us to church and a BBQ at their house after. You begged me to go, so of course I did. I was just beyond excited that you wanted me to go. I have heard some crazy things about this church; it's called "Church on the Move." One of my friends told me they are crazy like a cult. One of your dad's friends told me they automatically take your tithe out of your checking account without permission. I wasn't too worried about the money rumor, but the cult thing makes me nervous. You asked me to go, so cult or not, I am going.

The service was amazing! It's been a long time since I went to church and felt like I had been fed. I usually worship at a small church in Hagerman. It is . . . well, boring. I feel mean saying that, but I am usually thinking about my grocery list during the sermon. Every once in a while, I felt like I heard something just for me, but even then, it just doesn't hit me like this did. The entire service was overwhelming. The music was great. The sermon just soaked me in the love of Jesus. Then the altar call came. You and Katie both went forward. I cried and cried and cried. I know lives change when Jesus is asked in. I also know Satan attacks when you step toward Jesus. I know Jesus wins, but as you took those steps up and I saw the minister hug you and speak with you, I felt afraid. I know God has a plan for your life. I have always known that. My fear at this moment is greater than my happiness.

As I waited in the church for you, I prayed: *God, please help me to stop looking for the bad. Please help me to see the light in this darkness.* You really have been trying to do well. I know that. We have even had a few days when we got along. Maybe I am wrong. Maybe this is your first step toward God's plan. I really want to believe that. My life has me always looking for the next bad thing. I pray for God's help to see the good and quit waiting for the bad.

Finally, you came out, and we went to the barbeque. You swam and joked and played with Katie's little sisters. It made my heart happy to see you smiling. *OK, God, OK. I will enjoy the good moments when I can. This is a good moment. Thank you, Lord.*

Looking forward to your good moments, sweet girl. I love you.

Mom

# April 23, 2016

Lilly,

So, this month has been full of good times. You seem happy. Genuinely happy. I guess really the word I need is *joyful*. Since we went to church that first time, you just seem to be full of joy most of the time. There are still moments when I see you drift away and wander for a moment, but you come back right away, and there is joy. This, of course, means that I am so happy . . . and walking on eggshells . . . waiting. I keep praying that I would stop worrying and feel peace, but I can't turn off my brain. On the 15th, we went to watch the performance of *The Little Mermaid* at Roswell College. Your friend Haley was in it; she played one of the mermaid sisters. It was great. We enjoyed the show and of course, I enjoyed spending time with you. I just feel like I can't get enough. I know it's silly to still be writing these letters that you will probably never see, but I always have so much to say to you that just won't come out. Or if I try to speak, it's all wrong or you don't want to listen. It's too hard to battle all that right now. So, I walk on eggshells, I observe everything you do, and I write letters to pretend like we are close and talking and that everything is great. I'm sure a psychologist would consider my avoidance and denial interesting to discuss, but I don't really want to talk about it.

Back to why I am writing. Tonight you went to prom. This sweet boy, Adam I think, asked you. He came by and met your dad and everything. He seems very nice. You looked beautiful. We found this great dress at Once Again, a small consignment store in Roswell. The dress was a black and gray marble-looking fabric. It fit you perfectly. My worry started when you came home by nine-thirty and then changed and left. Not with the boy who took you to prom, but you left in your own car . . . going to pick up who knows, to do who knows—all while I lay here and assumed the worst. Before drugs I would just think you were out drinking and flirting with boys (yes, even I know that is putting it mildly), but still . . . I long for those days when drinking and boys were my biggest worry. Now, I constantly have a movie of you overdosing playing in my head. I am sure that my brain is absolutely making this worse, but I don't know how to control it. I am lying here writing this letter because I don't know what else to do. I keep staring at my phone like you're going to call me for some reason. I guess I am hoping. I don't know. . . . It's not that late yet. It's just now twelve, and your dad said you had to be home by two. I swear the clock is in slow motion . . .

It's 1:45 a.m., and you just came in. You came home . . . and you're even on time. Maybe my worry is silly. Maybe I need to quit worrying. Now to figure out how . . .

I love you. I am going to sleep now. Thank you for coming home.

Mom

# May 13, 2016

I am at a loss for words. I know you're using again. I see it every time we talk. You're losing what little weight you had. You are never where you say you are. The problem is I have absolutely no proof at all whatsoever, so I am the crazy person. Your dad is totally pissed at me for accusing you. Tanner is mad because you and I fight ALL the time. You have been mad at me for a year now. I am home with my family, and I am completely alone. I have been going to church every Sunday since Easter alone. I go and as soon as the first worship song starts, I cry. I cry silently through every song as I say the words. I feel God's comfort like I never have before. Every sermon is telling me to keep going. Every sermon is a whisper from God saying this will be ok. I hear it, I even know it deep down. I just don't know how to let go completely. I want to. I want to give all of this anger, disappointment, depression, sadness, worry, guilt, and every horrible thought to God and leave it at his feet. But I take it back every single time. I am thankful you brought me to this church. I feel at home here. I feel God carrying me through this.

There was a talent show at school today. You came to me this morning and said you were singing. So I took my class to watch and had my phone ready and recorded the most depressing/beautiful performance I've ever seen. When the music started, my heart sank.

A few weeks back when I first suspected you were using again, I heard a song on the radio that explained my feelings perfectly. I must have mentioned it to you. It was called "Burning House" by a country singer who goes by the stage name Cam. She talks about laying down next to someone she loved in a burning house. She couldn't save them. So she laid down beside them and held them close, and they burned together. Your voice was angelic as you sang words that explained my misery. I will lay here and burn with you baby girl. I love you and I can't let you do this alone. I can't.

Your eyes met mine as you sang the chorus. The chorus of that song is the soundtrack that haunts my dreams of overdoses and funerals.

This is the song you chose to sing at the talent show. I never cry in front of people. Hiding my miserable childhood from everyone around makes it hard to show emotion to the world. Even when my mother died, I didn't cry until I was alone with your dad on the drive home. But hearing you sing this song, at this time, I broke. Tears ran down my face as I tried to record you singing. My sweet little first graders stared at me and hugged me and kept asking if I was ok. I want to be ok. I don't want this song to explain the misery that is literally eating me from the inside out. Everyone sees it. My best friend at work hears me cry as we pray every morning. My co-workers reach out and touch my arm as I walk by to let me know I am not alone. And then I come home, and everyone is angry, and no one sees anything. You won the talent show. God blessed you with a beautiful singing voice and confidence I wish I had. My heart wrenches at the future you could have...instead of the one you're choosing.

I have no words.

Just silent prayers accompanied by tears.

I love you more.
Mama

# June 9, 2016

I woke up this morning with a rock in my stomach. I knew it before I saw it. You snuck out again, and you didn't come back home. I can't say that "you ran away." It makes me want to vomit. I just cried again and when I told your dad, I saw his face fill up with guilt. He didn't believe me. He was so angry with me for accusing you of using. Now, he looks at me with guilt and hurt beyond anything I've seen so far. He really believed his little girl was over this. He hoped so much, and now his hope is shattered. I just hug him, and he holds me as I cry. We hold each other together when we both want to give up and fall apart.

Seeing his disappointment takes me back to my childhood. My mother would always do this. She would get clean and come back wanting to be mother of the year. My brother would always get so excited. "Yay, we are finally gonna have a mom," he would say—every time, but I always knew better. I knew she would leave again. I knew she would try to stay clean, but the men and the drugs always won. So I waited and watched. I didn't want to be right about you; I didn't want to see you gone again; I didn't want you to choose the drugs over your family. I keep telling myself that you are not my mother. My mother didn't have much of a support system growing up. Her father was killed when she was thirteen. She was the only girl with four brothers . . . so yes, her daddy was her entire world. After he passed away, my grandmother stayed drunk for many years. My mother took care of her brothers the best she could, and the drugs helped. She grew, and so did her addiction. No one really saw what was going on in her life. No one stepped in to tell her she mattered. I keep praying that we will be able to break that cycle with you. We love you. We are here for you no matter what. You matter to us more than words can say.

I called the police to report you missing—again. They don't really care. Apparently, it isn't against the law for kids to run away in New Mexico. They didn't do much last time either, but I was in too much of a fog to really notice. A cop finally showed up about an hour after I called. He got your info, and I told him you had your phone this time, but you weren't answering. He told me they would be able to ping it and maybe that would help find you. After a few minutes, they said they had a location. In Hagerman. Out on Palimino road. Andrea's house . . . I should have known. He tells us they are sending an officer. We shouldn't go out there. So we waited . . . and waited. Eventually, they tell us they spoke with Andrea and that she hasn't seen you; I got mad and told that the cop she was lying. You're hiding. He reminds me that running away isn't against the law, so they can't search for you. They can only look with permission. I want to punch him in the face.

So, here I am. Going to bed . . . writing another stupid letter you won't read. This time I am prepared. I have some sleeping

June 9, 2016

pills. I hope that I sleep and that I don't dream. I am so tired of throwing dirt on your grave. I just want to sleep and see nothing, feel nothing, be nothing.

I am tired, baby girl. I love you, but I am tired. Too tired to be mad. Too tired to stay up all night and worry. I'm sorry. I just can't.

Love,
Mom

# June 11, 2016

Well it's the end of the day and your home. The last two days have been miserable. Not for you obviously. After barely speaking or listening to the police, you passed out on the bed and slept like the dead. Coming down, I suppose. I just sat there and stared at you sleep for a while. So many thoughts running through my head.

I had posted on social media that you had taken off again. We got up yesterday and sat around the house trying to stay busy. Your brother made a hundred phone calls asking if anyone had seen you. Then he took off to hang out with friends. He is so angry at you. It breaks my heart to see him like that. I can't help him anymore than I can help you. This situation is impossible. Your dad and I went to lunch at Piccolino's. We just sat there staring out the windows; then my phone rang. It was a kid named Ryan. He said he knew where you were, and he would tell me if I gave him cash. I just handed the phone to your dad. I heard your dad finish the conversation with him. He said he would give him fifty dollars if we found you. I hate everything.

We went to a small apartment complex in Artesia. Ryan told us what vehicle you had been in and which apartment to look for. We parked right next to the pickup you had been hiding in. Dad pointed out the apartment. We waited and watched for a bit. This place seems sketchy enough, all right. A few neighbors were sitting outside talking and laughing. Your dad got out of the pickup and went over to them. He showed them your picture and asked about the apartment you were supposed to be in. They said they had seen three people go in—two men and a girl, but the girl did not look like you. Dad asked them to keep an eye out for you and then gave them his phone number. Then he went to the door and knocked. A small lady answered.

She could have easily been mistaken for a young girl, just because of her size. Dad showed her your picture, and she said she had never seen you. Dad tried to look around her inside the apartment, but she just slammed the door in his face. He went back over and spoke with the neighbor guys who had been watching. I was sitting in the pickup the entire time just watching and praying. I was afraid for your father. What if some jerk pulled a gun on him. This place looked like it was full of drug dealers and murderers. The neighbor guys seemed nice enough. I knew good people lived here too. I grew up in places like this. I know my anger is forming my judgements about this place. I am just hating the world at this point. Your dad came back to the pickup and told me that both guys were very helpful and said they would call immediately if they saw you. Then we drove home. Without you.

Ryan called again a few hours later to ask for his money. Your dad told him we didn't find you. Ryan swears you were there. He even said he just saw you right before he called us. Dad told him to bring you to us if he wanted money. He agreed. I

## June 11, 2016

was surprised at first; then I remembered how badly he wanted money. He was strung out too, I bet. He needed another fix. Your dad and Ryan made a plan to meet today. This morning, your dad drove to Artesia. I stayed home. I couldn't handle another disappointment if you weren't there. You were. Ryan took your dad to that same apartment he had told us about. He walked in, and you were sitting on the couch—wearing a ball cap and dressed like a boy. He said you looked right at him and didn't even recognize him until he started yelling at you. He grabbed you by the arm and took you out of the house. He gave Ryan fifty dollars and left.

Now you're home. Sleeping. I just don't know what to do, where to turn, what to think or feel. How do you save your child from themselves? Is this what God thinks when he looks at us? Oh how he must feel as he watches us trip and fall over and over. Suddenly, I think I understand his love for me. For mankind. As I look at you passed out on the bed, so skinny and looking horrible, I feel this overwhelming love. I want to crawl into bed and wrap my arms around you and somehow make you feel my love and my protection. I want you to know that no matter how bad things get, no matter what decisions you make, I will still be here ready to help, hug, and love you. My heart swells: my eyes fill with tears and suddenly, I hear His whisper, "Just love her."

In an instant I know my place in this journey of yours. My job is to just be here and love you. I can't make you behave. I can't worry you into safety. I can be here and love you no matter what happens. Instead of making you feel horrible and fighting with you, I need to make sure that you know you are loved and that you always have a home. Thank You, Jesus, for answering my wordless cries. Thank You for giving me clarity and peace. Thank You for bringing my baby home.

I am not sure what happens now, baby girl, but I love you. I am here.

Always,
Mom

# July 6, 2016

Sweet girl,

June was a whirlwind of decisions after that last disappearing act of yours. We are headed to Tucson, Arizona. I am not sure what will happen there. I pray this is the answer we have been seeking. I pray this is the end of this chapter and the beginning of happiness. We shall see . . .

After your great escape last month, I started looking at rehabs. I was blown away at the waiting list everywhere . . . unless a person is on Medicaid. Then they could get you in right away. We make too much money to get help for you, but not enough to send you to a fancy place. Well, hell. After so much prayer and lots of frustration, my friend Stephanie mentioned a place she had heard about at church. It is called Teen Challenge. She told me she had been speaking to a friend about my situation, and they told her to tell me about Teen Challenge.

So I went online and started looking. They have facilities all over. I found several programs that were a year long, but the price was way beyond our capabilities. Then I found Springboard, which is located in Tucson. It seemed impossible as I read about it. Tucson is eight hours away by car—no way can we afford to fly. Tuition seemed high; it's $4,000 a month. I kept reading, and I just knew this was the place, even if we couldn't afford it. The program is four to six months long depending on the girl; it is a teen girls-only program. As I read, I felt this overwhelming peace come over me. I had no idea how God planned to pull this off, but I knew this was part of His plan. So I called. The intake lady I spoke with, Marla, was very nice. She explained the whole intake process and then she said the words that won me over, "We can get her placed in the facility in two weeks." Every other place I had spoken with had a wait of six months to a year. I just couldn't fathom how I could keep you alive or at home for another six months. Now I was hearing two weeks! She explained that she needed to do a phone interview with you. We set it up, and it went amazingly well. You didn't really seem too interested in this process of finding rehab, but you seemed ready to talk when it was time for this interview. Thank You, God. Wow. After your interview, Marla called me and we spoke about what needed to be done between the call and July 7, your intake date. Doctor appointments, dentist, shopping, oh and $4,000. My heart sank, and I wanted to say, "Ha! Never mind," but I said, "We will see you July 7." Then I hung up and cried. Where on earth would I get $4,000 in two weeks?

Then God showed me. He showed me what amazing friends we have. We started a GoFundMe account. People heard your story and helped. Most of them gave us support, encouraging words, and soon we had exactly $4,000. We went to the appointments. We bought the items on the list.

I felt like I was walking in quicksand. My feet were so heavy, and I just couldn't get moving. I was doing everything that needed

JULY 6, 2016

to be done, but I just felt disconnected. I watched everything from afar—in awe. Was this really going to happen?

This morning we all got up early. We have an eight-hour drive ahead of us. We are taking you to meet this very nice Marla lady and get you the help I have prayed for. We are on the road now. You and your brother are asleep in the back seat. I am hopeful for the first time since October of last year. I know your habit began before that, but October 25 was when I finally opened my eyes and saw that meth was stealing my daughter away. God has given me hope, and I can breathe.

I love you more.
Mom

# July 7, 2016

This morning we went to Springboard. We met Ms. Marla. She is wonderful. So sweet and caring. We met several other ladies; their names are a blur right now. We saw the other girls living in the house. They all seem too young to be fighting this battle . . . just like you. The house you're staying in is beautiful. You're not allowed any contact with the outside world at all for a month. You will be able to call us for the first time on August 8. Then we can send letters, and you can call once a week after that. They don't allow internet or cell phones; even secular music is forbidden. This place is all God and His love all the time. I know this is my answer. I know this is God's will.

The quicksand was gone by the time we started driving here yesterday. But just when I think I have gone through the hardest part of this, I learn differently. Driving away and leaving you in a place with people I don't know and placing my trust in strangers . . . the ache is beyond anything I can describe. I know this is good . . . but driving away, my heart and body feel like they are in pieces. I am glad we decided to drive home tomorrow. We are in the motel right now. You are just right up the road. I am fighting the urge to drive back and bring you home. I just keep crying. I can't turn off the tears. Your dad and brother went down to the pool. I think they just couldn't stand to see me cry anymore.

You are starting a new chapter. I need to start a new chapter too. I have to learn to trust God completely and stop worrying. I need to find happiness again. I need to get out of this miserable, funky, fog I have been in since October.

I will after we get home. Tonight, I cry because you're up the road. Tomorrow, I will cry because I am leaving you in another state. I am only able to do this because I know that God is with you. You are right where He needs you to be.

> *For I know the thoughts that I think toward you, says the Lord, thoughts of peace and not of evil, to give you a future and a hope.*
>
> —Jeremiah 29:11

I know He has plans for you, baby girl. I know. I love you more.

Mom

# August 8, 2016

Tonight, I heard your voice for the first time in a month! You sounded wonderful. Beautiful. You sounded like my daughter again. It has been so long since I have spoken to this girl. We put you on speaker so you could talk to us all. You didn't say a lot. Just that things were good. It sounds like you have made some amazing friends with some of the other girls. You really seem to like your counselor, Ms. Suzi. You speak very highly of her. You're only allowed ten minutes to talk to us. Of course, it flies by so very fast. After we hung up, I just kept smiling. It was really great to get a glimpse of the girl I have been missing for so long.

I too have been busy while you're gone. A few things have changed. First, I am finally sleeping again. I really didn't think I would with you being in a different state, but I have slept amazingly well every night since we took you to Springboard—and without medicine. I feel very peaceful most of the time. I started a prayer group on Tuesday nights. I just put it on Facebook, and people came. We meet at the community center in town. About six ladies attend regularly. I am so happy. It makes me feel so much better to have people to talk with and pray with. Of course, school has started, so I am super busy with that also. My friend Sarah and I still pray every morning, but I don't cry every time—only once in a while. I think that's an improvement. Life seems to be looking up. I want to be completely happy and let the past go, but every now and then, I get a flash of a daydream of you gone again. Of you coming home and getting lost in the misery again. Of you overdosing . . . I try to let it go, but it's always there in the background noise. I keep praying and asking God to take it. I will keep praying until the whisper is gone. I heard your sober voice today. I heard you laugh, and it made my heart smile. God will carry you through this, and I will let him carry me too. I just need to get rid of that shadow of fear.

I love you so much, baby girl. I am praying every minute for you and your recovery.

I love you more,
Mom

# August 18, 2016

I took off from work today. We are driving to Tucson, Arizona, to see you . . . our first visit! I am beyond excited! It's just dad and me. We are coming to attend a class with you and then do a family counseling session. I don't really know what it's all about, and I don't really care. After it's over, we get to take you for an hour and go eat. I miss you so very much. We have spoken every Monday night since that first call. You sound great. You talk a lot about what you are learning. I am amazed at the time spent studying the Bible. You even said you have read a book! Haha, you hate to read, but I guess without TV and cellphones that is all you can do.

Who knew all I had to do to get you to read was lock you away from the world?! It was a book about the story of Ruth in the Bible. I always thought that was a great story. Even after losing everything, she sticks by her mother-in-law. Ruth truly loves her and wants to be by her side. I don't know what it's like to have family like that. My dad left when I was little. I don't have any memory of him until I met him again at fourteen. My mom . . . well, she could barely take care of herself, much less two kids. My grandma took us when I was ten, and she was always there, after the bar closed. I love her, and I am grateful for her taking us, but I don't know that I would use the words *loving family* to describe us. Honestly, your dad and you kids are the most loving family I've ever known. I did live with my dad and stepmom and sisters for a few years in high school, and they showed me what a "normal" family looked like. They tried to love me like I belonged there, but I was too angry to accept that love. I needed time to grow up.

I pray that our family has that deep-rooted love that Ruth showed for Naomi—the love that God gives us for each other. I know how much I love all of you; I just worry that because I don't always show it that I will push you guys away. Let's be real . . . I worry about everything. I am working on that. God is dealing with me on several issues, and the big one right now is trusting Him and not worrying. It's hard to let go of the worry . . . what will I do with my spare time . . . Haha? I don't know whether that's funny or sad.

Ugh! I am getting way too deep in this letter. We are in the middle of nowhere driving to see my baby girl. I am happy! I cannot wait to wrap my arms around you and just hug you . . .

See you soon!

Mom

# Later That Same Day

Oh you look beautiful. You're smiling. You're talking to us. The class we sat through was really good. It taught us about love languages. How you can use other people's love languages to speak to them in a way they understand. You and your dad have the same love language.

Wow... shocker! Haha... I am the only one with the language of touch. You two share time as your love language. I'm not surprised. You are so much like him. After the class, we spoke with your counselor, Ms. Suzie. She is a beautiful soul. She spoke highly of you. She said you took responsibility for all your decisions. You made it clear that you had great support from your family. I am so glad to hear that. We try to make sure you know that we love and support you—that we want what is best for you. After our meeting, they announced that you are being baptized. Ms. Suzie asks your dad if he would be the one to do it. She speaks of the growth you have made ... of your decision to follow Jesus. Your dad stands next to you, glowing with pride and happiness. I am so blessed to see this. I know this day is real, but it feels so dreamlike. I think I almost forgot how to just trust this and enjoy it. We are finally allowed to take you to dinner. You have to be back in two hours. I was a little sad to hear that. We had driven eight hours, but spending any time with you is worth it. We ate and talked and laughed. We took a selfie or two. You called and talked to your brother. It was a great day. My heart was happy. Now Dad and I are sitting in the motel room.

You are back at Springboard with the other girls and the house parents. We will drive home tomorrow. I keep praying my thank-yous to the Lord, but I feel like they aren't enough. I am overwhelmed with the love and happiness I feel just seeing you and all that you're learning. My mind keeps going back to our talk with Ms. Suzie. She said something today that literally blew my mind. Today, Ms. Suzie said, "We teach our students here that addiction is not a disease."

You can be saved from addiction. Jesus can break that chain of bondage and set you free. What? This statement rocked my foundation.

My whole life I had believed that addiction was a disease. It excused my mom for all her bad decisions. My mom believed in Jesus. We had many great letter exchanges discussing God and Jesus at length. When she was in jail and clean, her faith was strong. I know she died still in her addiction. I always thought it was because she had a disease. I grew up surrounded by addicts. They couldn't quit. They had a disease, didn't they? Was I wrong about this my whole life? I mean I believe in God. I have prayed a lot, especially this last year. I see how your life is changing. I have seen God change my life. My selfishness. My bad decisions. I lost my marriage. I lost my way. God turned it around. For sure. God changed me. Could he really break all bonds of addiction? Is there really a chance that my daughter could get out of this and break this curse? My hope is high . . . my doubt is there though. It's hard not to hear that little voice saying, *Watch out* or *It's too good to be true*. Oh, I hate that voice . . . I really, really hate that voice. I want this to be true. For you, baby girl, I want God to break these chains.

I love you,
Mom

# September 9, 2016

Dear Lilly,

Here we are on the road again. Driving to Tucson. This time we get an overnight visit. I am so excited. Your brother and cousin Christian are with us. They are also excited to see you. We all miss you so much. The house is quiet but less sad now that we know where you are. At least I feel less sad. I still wake up in a panic occasionally . . . still wake up searching for you. It takes a minute for me to remember that you're safe. You're not high. You're not being taken to some foreign country to be sold. These nightmares haunt me. I pray that someday they will go away. They pop up less often during the day, but at night . . . sometimes the fear is paralyzing. Tanner and Christian are in the backseat talking and laughing. It just feels so normal. Oh, I pray we are on the road to normal.

# September 10, 2016

We checked into the motel and headed over to Springboard. It always calms my soul to see you. Oh, your smile is beautiful. You are happy to see your brother and Christian. My heart is soaring at the sight of you three talking. We say hello to everyone and get you signed out. We decide to go to the mall and walk around. You look happy. You look like you . . . I can't stop smiling. We go bowling where you three laugh and dance and have fun. I just keep watching you. Making sure this is real. We finally get back to the motel and of course you all want to swim. I go down with you and enjoy the sounds of you laughing along with Tanner and Christian. Then the panic. I wanted to go up to the room; you three did not. Part of my brain knows you're safe with Tanner.

He always looks out for you. The other part, the part that stays terrified constantly, doesn't trust anyone. I want to. I want to know that I can walk away and trust that you will not take off. I want to know you won't find drugs somehow. I hear how crazy I sound. I know it's insane. What I don't know is how to turn off the crazy. So, I walk away. I go upstairs. I try not to just stare out our window and watch you three. I shower and change and breathe and pray. I sit and stare out the window and pray again. Finally, I hear the three of you in the hallway, and I take a deep breath. I didn't realize how worried I was until I heard that sound. Oh, how on earth will I ever move past this?

I didn't sleep at all. I kept waking up to make sure you were still in the room. How will I act when you're home? How will I ever trust you again? If I can't trust you and you see me watching all the time, you will hate me. I don't want that. I just want to rewind and go back. I hate drugs. I want my daughter—the one who hugged me out of nowhere for no reason. The one who would lie on my bed and talk to me about her day. The one I trusted. The one who didn't have me living in constant fear.

Leaving you is awful and safe. I hate driving away. I am happy you're getting help that you need. I am so happy you are growing and learning about God. I see the changes in you. I hear them in the letters you send. I am thankful beyond words, but driving away is painful. I let tears fall silently down my cheeks. I don't want Tanner to know how hard this is for me. He already hangs onto so much anger. I try to talk to him about it, but he won't. He says he doesn't believe in God, so he feels like this rehab is ridiculous, but he sees the change in you. I know he is happy, but I also know he is afraid to hope.

I will continue to pray for you both—that you will break the chains of addiction and Tanner will find his way back to God.

I love you.

Mom

# September 30, 2016

So, today I spoke with Ms. Suzie on the phone. You are finished with your school curriculum. They are discussing your release from Springboard. I am ecstatic and terrified all in the same breath. You have only been there a few months. Is that enough time? Did we do enough? What will happen now?

I have been in church every Sunday crying and praying. I know that this is in God's hands. I know He has already told me just to love you and to trust Him. These are things I know, but the fear sits on the surface. The fear wants to hold me down. I hang up the phone and just sit. I breathe and pray. I feel the knot in my stomach grow. I am sitting here arguing with myself in my head. I know I have no control over this situation. I know I need to let go and trust. I also know that is easier said than done. I want to let go. I want to feel excited to have you home. But the fear is overwhelming. It is amazing how fear can completely take over and steal all rational thought. I don't sleep.

Dad and Tanner are so happy to hear the news. I try to pretend. I am too. I want to be happy. I want to have my daughter back. I want to leave you there. Where you're safe. Where the drugs are far away. Your dad and I have discussed moving from here. Moving to a place where you don't know anyone. We discussed selling our home and moving. We didn't do it . . . why? How can I bring you back here—back to the place that ruined your life? Back to the friends who kept you high and kept you hidden when you ran away? I know my reaction is wrong. I know this is not the way I should feel. I know God my Father is disappointed, but I don't know how to fix it. How do I get rid of this blanket of terror that is sitting on me cutting off my air supply? I pray.

I feel the weight lift. Not completely. Just enough that I can breathe. I know if I would let it go, God would take it all. But I'm stubborn. I keep hanging on. Even with my stubborn selfishness, God helps me breathe. He carries the weight that is so heavy for me. He gives me enough peace to sleep for a while. I know that rest is from Him because I wake feeling truly rested. Truly ready to face this next step. The fear is still there . . . on the outskirts . . . because I choose for it to stay . . . but I hear His whisper. It is time for the next chapter.

OK, baby girl. Time to come home.

# October 10, 2016

We are headed home. You are in the backseat laughing and chatting away. You look beautiful and happy. You have gained weight, and you look healthy. When we brought you to Springboard, you had no fat on your body at all. You were literally skin and bones. I am so relieved to see you with little rolls of fat over your pants. Funny the things I notice to feel better.

The girls were sad to see you go. It looks like you have made some wonderful friends who understand the hell you have gone through. Your teachers and counselors all hugged you and said they were proud. You were beaming. I am proud of the progress you made here. The things you learned. The faith you're walking away with.

I hope we are enough to keep you on this path. I hope I can take you to church enough to keep you focused on God. I don't know what life is going to look like at home. Do we put you in school? Dad and I can't decide. I spoke with the high school here in town, and they don't think it would be good to enroll you in the middle of a semester. They want us to wait until January.

Which means lots of days home alone. I am at work. Your dad is at work. Tanner is working and pretty much stays with friends. I spoke with my boss to see if you could just sit in my classroom and do online school . . . no contact with kids just sitting and working. Of course, he said no. It would be a distraction. He has no idea that no matter where you are, I am going to be distracted. My mind will be worried. My heart will be aching. Hopefully just long enough to see that you are OK. Maybe then I can move forward. Maybe then.

Ms. Suzie invited us to come back next month to speak at a dinner. I am excited to hear that . . . at least we will still be in contact with them. Surely, they have taught you all you need to know. I feel horrible that my mind is doubting. I know you have been leaning on God to get you through this program. To get you clean. How can I be worried about you when I know He is in charge? I wish I could say my faith is so strong that I have no fear. I'm scared. I'm scared that we will lose you again. I'm scared to trust.

# November 13, 2016

You have settled in. You started taking night classes at school in Artesia. You have been going and coming home on time. You seem to be doing well, but the doubt and fear are there. I notice little things . . . your makeup is super dark. Your smile just off. I think it's just me looking for reasons to be worried. You are always where you say you're going. You stay home most of the time.

Really you only leave for school and once or twice with friends—not the ones you were getting high with. These friends are the ones you had before the drugs took over. I want to be happy. I want to trust. We are leaving tomorrow to go to Tucson to speak at a dinner that is full of people who donate to Teen Challenge. I have been praying about what to say. Just a short speech about how our lives have been impacted. I don't know how to make that short. Before Teen Challenge, I was living in fear of burying my daughter because she overdosed. Now I have hope. Hope for a future without drugs. Hope for a future full of happiness and good decisions. You have to speak also. You said it would be just like giving your testimony. I guess you had to do that when you were there. You don't seem worried at all.

# November 14, 2016

We are here. It was a strange drive. You didn't talk much. In fact when we left, we prayed, and you burst into tears. I tried to talk to you about it. You just said you were nervous to be going back. I prayed. Ms. Suzi is letting us stay at her beautiful house. I love it here. We took some great pictures of you in her backyard. She had a barbeque, and her family all came over.

They were all so nice. I feel a little like we are intruding, but it is so nice to see them all so happy and enjoying each other's company. You seemed to be having a good time. Tomorrow is the dinner and the speeches. I am super nervous. You seem pretty peaceful about it all. I wish I could be like that. You always did love to be in the spotlight though. I remember the first time you sang at Old Timers day in Hagerman. You had been practicing for weeks. We bought you a pretty pink dress and signed you up for the talent show. You sang "The Climb" by Miley Cyrus.

Before you sang, I was so nervous I wanted to puke. You were totally fine. You got onstage and sang amazingly. A lady standing next to me asked who sang the original song. I told her, and she said she was going to buy it because of the way you sang. I was in tears. It was beautiful. I always loved hearing you sing, but that was the first time I really thought you could take that voice and have a career if you chose to. You didn't win, but you came in second. You won first place the next year. I miss hearing you sing. You used to sing the national anthem at football games and baseball games. I had to leave the first football game this year. As soon as the girl started singing the national anthem, I started crying uncontrollably. It was so embarrassing. I couldn't watch volleyball either. I went to a game and as soon as the girls came out onto the court, I started looking for you. I left and didn't go to another one. I know we are in a better place now than we were when school started, but it is still hard sometimes. I feel like I lost that girl, and now we are getting to know each other again. I don't know if that makes sense. I just know there are times when I miss my daughter. I'm glad you're back and doing better, but I don't think it will ever be the same. Maybe that is my fault. Maybe I have changed so much I can't go back. I don't know. I guess I need to quit writing and get some sleep. You are next to me snoring with your head under the covers.

I love you.

# November 15, 2016

We will head home in the morning. We both spoke tonight. You saw a couple of the girls that you knew from Springboard. The dinner was very nice. Your speech was short and sweet. You just said you felt like they had given you a second chance. I said pretty much the same. An older woman who had kids spoke; she had gone through their adult program. She had lost custody of her kids, and the program had helped her get them back and get on her feet. Her story hit me pretty hard. I wish my mom had found help like that. A couple of men also spoke; they had gone through the men's program and received some job training and really changed their hearts and lives. All these stories and so many lives changed. Teen Challenge really is an amazing program reaching so many. I was overwhelmed to see people who were in the various programs in Tucson. Teen Challenge is definitely doing God's work. I'm thankful that God sent us here. Whatever happens now is in His hands. I know that He loves you even more than I do. I can get through whatever comes.

# November 18, 2016

Last night you snuck out. You have your phone. You answered when I called. You just told me you were with friends, and you would be home later. I don't even know how to feel or what to say or anything. I feel stupid. I feel sad. Tanner doesn't even care. He said he is done caring. That breaks my heart. He has been with Christian all day. I am so thankful he has his cousin Christian to talk to. Today is Christian's birthday. I am hoping they go do something fun. Tanner won't talk to me. He knows that the anger he has makes me sad for him and you. Your dad hasn't said much. He just keeps watching me. He knows how close I was to the edge last time. I thought I was hiding it, but he saw everything. I am not as terrified as last time. I guess I'm getting used to it. What an awful thing to get used to.

I just got off the phone with you. It's one in the afternoon; I gave you till three to return. If you're not home by three, I'm calling to report you as a runaway again. The cops won't do anything. I'm just doing it so that if they happen to find your body after you overdose, they will contact us. This is what I told you on the phone. You didn't respond. You said you would be here before three. I feel like you won't. I know you're high again. I don't know how I know, but I do. I am so, so disappointed. I wanted God to say OK; that's enough.

I got in my car and went to the store just to have something to do. Dad and Tanner are working on his car in the shop. I just yelled at God:

> "Why? This isn't fair! I worked so hard to get out of this life, and now I am stuck in it again?! I did my time. I had a mom who didn't care. She stayed high and left me with her stupid boyfriends. I had a grandma who was too busy to pay attention. My brother fell into drugs and alcohol too. I ran away from that all and made a better life! Why? I don't feel like I deserve this."

As clear as day, I heard Him answer, "This isn't about you. Just love her."

Oh. Well I mean, yeah; I know not everything is about me. But do I . . . really? I guess I had taken all this on myself. I took all the hurt and pain and tried to carry it, didn't I? I mean had I even bothered to look at the other people around me and notice their pain? Did I reach out and try to help them? No. I had been so focused on me, me, me . . . wow. I guess I really need to change my perspective. It isn't about me.

Thank you, Jesus. Thank you for listening to my fit and giving me an answer anyway.

Three o'clock came and went. You called at three fifteen and said, "I'm sorry, Mom" and hung up. I called the Sheriff and reported you as a runaway. I know the police won't do

## November 18, 2016

anything. I know they don't care, but if I report you missing, they will know who to call if they find your body somewhere. I cried for a bit. I walked outside and helped your dad and brother work on the car. It isn't about me. I sat out there with them for a while. We were all sad, but we laughed a little while we talked about other things. We talked about anything except the thing we were all thinking about. You.

# November 19, 2016

I guess the drugs are hitting everyone right now. Christian's mom, Carla, took off last night. She left her husband and her children to go be with her dealer. At least that is what Christian said. On his birthday . . . well, technically right after his birthday, but that doesn't matter. It reminds me of my grandmother. She called me the day after my twenty-third birthday to tell me that she found out my mother had died. It doesn't matter that it was the day after; what matters is that I remember every year on my birthday. I don't know whether Christian will remember that his mom left him the day after his birthday every year, but this year it stinks. He spent the day talking to Tanner and playing video games. I am sad for him. I'm sad for us.

Our house is sad. I don't know where you are. We haven't heard from you since yesterday when you said sorry. I am praying a lot, but not scared. Not like before. Just sad. I know if we lose you that you are home. You will be in Heaven. I am not ready for that, but it does bring some comfort. I don't want to lose you. I don't want the drugs to win. But honestly that is all I think about. I am praying to be able to move past that, but I don't know how. Today is Saturday. I will spend today and tomorrow in bed. I will cry. I will pray. I will kick and scream and throw my fit.

Then on Monday I will go to work and move forward. One step at a time. We will help Christian deal with his situation. I wonder how Christian's sister Pheobe and his dad Ronald are handling all of this. I need to call Pheobe and check on her. It is her mom too. I need to, but I can't seem to make myself do much of anything.

I can pray. I will pray. I know God has a plan. I just wish I knew what it was . . .

# November 21, 2016

Today, you sent me a picture through snapchat. I had sent you messages everywhere I could think of—Facebook messenger, snapchat, email, whatever. Today, you responded with a picture of yourself and the words, "I miss you too." I'm not even sure how to feel. I mean I feel like I just got a proof of life picture from a kidnapper. You miss me too? Really? At least I know you're alive.

I will say this time feels different. I guess I keep thinking in terms of before rehab (BR) and after rehab (AR). In the story of Lilly, it's BR and AR . . . haha. Oh, my brain. Anyway BR, I was constantly afraid—to the point of not being able to function in real life. I mean I was functioning, but only going through the motions. Just one step at a time. One foot in front of the other. Not really here but still going. Now AR, I am sad, but I am here. I am feeling sad and disappointed, but more than that I feel hope. I know that you made a connection with Jesus while you were in rehab. I could see it in your face during our visits. I could hear it in your voice during our phone calls. Everyone could see it. You were glowing with the Holy Spirit. I know that. I know that God will eventually pull you out of this pit. My fear is that he will pull you out by taking you home. I don't know if I am ready for that. I went to church yesterday, like I do every Sunday. I just stand and sing during the worship and let the music hit me. I always cry. I cry every time. From the first note to the last. I cry and then I sit and listen to the pastor. His words are always exactly what I need to hear. I walk out feeling fed for the week. God really is amazing. He always gives me exactly what I need to keep pushing—to keep walking. I need a lot this week.

Thanksgiving is coming up. I know there is so much to be thankful for. But I'm so tired. We all are. Dad is trying so hard to keep us all going. He drags me around everywhere he goes. He looks over me constantly. Tanner is around . . . but barely. I am not even sure what he is doing. He comes in and out. We talk but never about anything important. Never you. He is so angry. He makes sure that I know he is OK and not doing anything stupid. Christian has pretty much been here since his mom left. Pheobe is staying with her friend Abby a lot. We are all struggling. Thanksgiving doesn't sound like a day I want to deal with. I don't know. It's in a few days. I guess we will see.

# November 25, 2016

You sent another picture today. Thanks. I never know what to think or how to feel. I always feel relief. You're alive. I take a deep breath and thank Jesus. Yesterday was Thanksgiving. We didn't do anything. We went to Nana's for a bit. It was so hard for me. Everyone just went on like it was a normal day. I tried—tried to pretend. I guess I did a good job. Dad smiled and looked at me like he was happy to see me talking and even laughing a little. I just think of the gaping hole without you there.

I am sure Christian and Pheobe feel that way about their mom not being there. Just missing. I guess she is with some guy named Rudy in the next town over. Christian has talked with me and Tanner quite a bit. Today was the first day I saw Pheobe. She was just herself, but with a sadness about her. I understand that. I hate drugs. It just seems that has always been a thorn in my side. Just a stabbing, throbbing, hateful thorn. My mom was always using something as far back as I can remember—drugs or alcohol—she used whatever she had on hand. All my uncles used drugs. Only Martin stayed away from the heavy stuff. Just used pot. My grandma stayed drunk until I was in high school. Then my brother joined in the family tradition. I tried pot. Not a big fan. Drank a little bit for a little while until the fear slapped me that it was becoming a daily thing. Honestly, fear of becoming my mother is what kept me sober. I never tried anything hard. I was afraid of being the one-time user and hooked person. That is what happened to you. You explained to me during one of the therapy sessions that you were hooked from the second you tried meth. One time and it sucked you in. Sucked you in and stole you away from us. Changed my baby girl into this wild woman that I don't know.

Ugh. This month is almost over. December will be a slap in the face. Your birthday. Christmas. More time to spend with family and no you. I just want to skip it. I need to pray. I need to ask God to help me stop being wrapped in myself and to focus on my family. I know I am not alone in my pain. But it is so hard to see past it. I feel hope. I feel God's presence so close, but it is next to impossible to step outside my pain and see others.

Writing letters to you helps; it helps me say the things I can't say to anyone else. I am still going along with everyday life. I still get out of bed and make myself face the day. I do think I am doing better than BR; I do a little more than going through the motions. I allow myself to have some feelings. Like a brick wall with one brick missing. Only a little bit is able to get through—enough that I can survive until God sends the answer to my prayers. He sustains me with every church service, every friend who offers encouragement, every picture you send, and every time I hear from you. God is good even when this world feels like it is going to fall in and crush me.

Even then.

I love you, baby girl. I miss you. All the time.

# December 17, 2016

Happy birthday. You are seventeen. I don't know where you are. I don't know who you are with. I don't know what you are doing. I want to sleep all day. Sarah called and invited me to the movies. We have been wanting to see *Fantastic Beasts* for a while. Dad is pushing for me to go. He knows I am barely hanging on today. Maybe I will. Tanner is asleep and probably will be all day. He came in about four thirty this morning. Dad is at work. I keep staring at my phone like you will magically call or appear or something. Yeah, I'm going. Maybe a movie will make my brain shut up.

Well, it's almost midnight. Not a word from you today. Not a picture. Nothing. You turned seventeen, and I didn't even get to talk to you. I have hugged you every birthday for sixteen years, and now I can't. My heart is hurting. I pray that wherever you are God sends someone who tells you, "Happy birthday and your momma loves you." I pray you know that I thought about you all day. I longed to pull you into my arms and breathe in your scent. Every fiber of my body aches for my baby girl. I am thankful that you are out there, and someday I may be able to hug you again.

Please, God, please.

# December 21, 2016

I got a picture today. I'm glad. I was beginning to panic a little. I try so hard to give my fear over to God, but it is not easy. It eases my mind a little when I hear from you. I mean the only thing you say is, "I love you," but that is enough. I know you're alive and you think of us. That is enough.

# December 23, 2016

Today I heard your voice. It was a horrible day, but you finally called me, and I broke the awful news to you. Your Uncle Ronald took his own life today. Christian is the one who found him hanging from a tree. He cut him down and called his nana. I was at school finishing up some work stuff when she called me. I called Dad. We all made it out to the house fast. It still doesn't seem real. Pheobe was planning to go to Texas with her friend, and she found out right before they left. I spoke with her on the phone. It was awful. I told Christian to come home with me, and I told Carla not to come down because right now, everyone blames her. It was a horrible, terrible, awful day.

I couldn't reach you at all. I called your friend Nicole. She had helped hide you before, so I thought maybe she knew where to reach you. She got in touch with you, and you called. Then I told you. I hate the words I had to say. I hate the heartbreak I see everywhere. Yesterday, my heart was hurting the most. Today, my heart hurts, but there is so much heartbreak around that my usual hurt seems small. You are here on this earth. You are alive, and I still have hope. Today, Nana lost her son. Your dad lost his brother. Carla lost a husband. Christian and Pheobe lost their dad. Mine is small.

Ronald was heartbroken and angry when Carla left. He burned all her stuff. He became even quieter than before. He was lost. Then he started seeing some girl we called Kat. Another girl strung out on drugs, but so was he. I guess she was into heroin. He started using it too. We were all worried, but what do you do? We didn't know the specifics of what was going on. We knew he looked worse. His behavior was strange even for him. He was working but partying hard on his days off. At this point Christian was pretty much with us all the time. Pheobe was with Abby or at Nana's most of the time. She stayed with Ronald when she could. She loves her daddy. Loved. She loved her daddy. I guess he was supposed to take Carla out on a date tonight. And then his boss said he was stealing from her and refused to pay him. I'm not sure what happened next.

Christian was working for a neighbor with Nana picking up pecans. He was running to the house for a bathroom break. He drove up to the house and saw his dad. I have spent the day in prayer for everyone. I am not sure what will happen now. We plan a funeral. We try to move forward. I have a new focus. I love you. I have to push aside my worries and sadness and focus on Pheobe and Christian. I can't stay wrapped up in my sadness anymore. I heard your voice today. It was an awful conversation. But I heard your voice today. And I can hear it again tomorrow. We won't hear Ronald's again. Not on this earth. My heartbreak is small compared to that.

Love,
Mom

# December 25, 2016

Today is Christmas day. A broken and sad Christmas. It has been a year of heartache. Somehow, everyone was invited to come to our house. Maybe we had planned it before Ronald . . . I honestly can't remember. None of us feel like Christmas. I think we would all just like to sleep through the rest of this year. But being together helps. I woke up with a prayer.

> God, thank You for the birth of Your son. Thank You for the sacrifice He made to save us. Thank You for loving us when I know we don't deserve You. Thank You for Your grace. Please, Lord, carry us through this day. Help us to find happy moments in all the darkness.

Of course, he answered. Of course.

We didn't do a lot, but we hung out. We watched movies. We ate. We told stories about Ronald and Toby when they were little. We laughed. We joked. It was forced by us all. I know everyone was missing Ronald. I was thinking of you. I was worried about how you took the news. I was scared my turn was coming—my turn to bury my baby. I kept waiting for the knock on the door. The call. I am afraid a lot, but something about today has really made it louder . . . more present. Probably because it is Christmas. You were supposed to be here.

After rehab and life-changing events, you were supposed to be home celebrating with us. But you're not. We found out that you're in Texas . . . with strangers. Pheobe is in Lubbock with her friend Abby. I think they arranged to see you at the mall or something. Pheobe said you looked good . . . I wonder if she has any clue how bad things have been with you. It's not like we have discussed it or anything. Debbie, Abby's mom, said she questioned the guy you were with . . . name, address, all that. I suppose she thought we would want to know. At this point, it does no good. We aren't looking. We aren't chasing like we did before. We are just waiting—for what I'm not sure. Maybe for you to come home. To change your mind. To get clean. Or the other . . . to die. What horrible words I write on Christmas night . . . but truthful. I see this ending in one of those ways . . . I hope. So tomorrow we get up and plan a funeral. Maybe you will show up . . . if you call, so I can tell you. Maybe we plan yours soon after.

Man, I'm tired. Tired of waiting.

God, please let me find a way to move forward. I feel like I am stuck in quicksand. The sand is steadily pulling on my feet harder and harder, but somehow, I keep taking one step at a time.

Somehow, I am still moving forward. There are moments that it feels impossible to pick up my feet and go, but I always manage to do it. No, not me . . . God is picking up my feet. God is pulling me through the sand. I know this. I guess I needed to remind myself. I guess that is why I keep writing these ridiculous letters that you will never read. I am writing them so I can say

## December 25, 2016

what is on my mind, in my heart, on my soul. I need to get it out into the world without dumping it on anyone else. Reading this I realize how I am focused only on myself. Your dad and brother have been hit hard by this situation too . . . and now that Ronald took his own life, your cousins Christian and Pheobe are thrown into our house, our mess. I pray I can be helpful to them. I pray I can start focusing on your dad and brother. I have to get focused on them not me.

Oh . . . OK, God. I hear You.

> *"Let each of you look out not only to his own interests, but also for the interests of others."*
> —Philippians 2:4

I have been very focused on me. I need to start looking outward and helping others. Step 1. Help everyone plan a funeral.

I love you, girl. So much more.

# December 30, 2016

Today, we buried Ronald Jay Couper. He was thirty-seven years old. He wasn't old enough. Nana's uncle Glen sang *Amazing Grace*. A lot of people came because they had known Ronald since his childhood. The family was all OK until Nana asked your dad to lower the ashes into the hole. Then your dad broke. Just a little. His eyes started to tear; then we all fell apart. It absolutely ripped me apart to see your dad hurt over his little brother. I was amazed at how well Christian and Pheobe held together. I mean they were upset, of course, but they made it through. Afterward, we went to the community center.

There was a ton of food, and all the family was there. Well, almost all; you weren't. I haven't spoken with you since I told you. I let Nikki know the date of the funeral, but I have no idea if she told you. Anyway of course, there was tension with the family. Some of the nieces blame Carla for Ronald's decision. Some of us know it was the drugs. I think he just pushed too hard at the end. I think he got into some stuff he knew he couldn't get away from.

One bad decision leads to another and then on and on. So many lives shattered. I think Christian and Pheobe will eventually be OK. They are strong kids with good heads on their shoulders. I'm not sure about your Aunt Carla. She has been here all day for the funeral stuff . . . she just wants it to be all about her and her pain. I'm not sure she will ever get over this. I see that in my pain over you I have been just as selfish as she is. I have been so worried about my brokenness that I haven't been looking to help anyone else.

The kids have moved in. Pheobe took your room. Christian is sharing with Tanner. We put most of your stuff in the closet.

We still need to finish getting their things from their house. I am not sure how it works, but I am talking to your dad about getting legal guardianship over them. Christian just turned seventeen, but Pheobe is barely fifteen. I don't want to worry about dealing with Carla if anything happens. She is pretty strung out herself. Who knows if I will even be able to reach her if there is an emergency. I hate drugs! I feel like I am surrounded by them.

I will focus on the kids. And on Tanner and your dad. I can't stay in my pain anymore. I just can't.

I love you, and it's so strange that I feel like if I stand up and move on, I am giving up on you. That seems so stupid now that I read it. I won't ever give up on you. I will pray you through this. I will cherish the moments when I hear from you. I will rejoice the moment you come back to us. God knows your path. He will guide you back.

Until then, I have to quit going through the motions and get back to living. I love you, baby girl.

I miss your face.

# January 8, 2017

Today, we started back to school. I had in-service yesterday, and of course, we had a big talk about suicide. Sometimes, I feel like they treat teachers like students. It was awkward and uncomfortable for me. I knew everyone there knew about Ronald committing suicide, so of course, now they were all getting lectured because I work there too?! I don't know. People deal with these things so strangely sometimes.

I was worried about Christian and Pheobe heading back to school. It seems weird to go on with life, but they both said they were ready. They were tired of doing nothing, and they both said they had a good day. And just like that life goes on. We lose someone we love, and the world keeps turning. I realize now looking back that I really did stay stuck in the sand over this situation with you. Maybe not stuck . . . just walking very slowly.

I look back on the last year and see how much God has carried me through. I am so very grateful you introduced me to this church. Every Sunday I go and cry through the worship service. I feel every word the pastor says, and I walk out feeling like I can breathe again. Your dad has been going too. Every Sunday, he is there. I see some changes in him too.

God is good. I know God is working on you too wherever you are and whatever you are doing. I am praying hard for your brother too; he has taken this thing with you so much harder than I realized. He doesn't come home much. When he does, he is usually high . . . I hope just from pot, but I don't ask. He just has so much anger.

I got a picture from you the other day. It just said, "I love you too." You look OK. Of course, now with filters and all that junk, who knows what is truly behind the picture. More than anything it shows me you're still alive. That was my main concern. It shows me you still know we are here and that we love you. That means something too.

As I go out into the world now, I notice so many lost faces—so many people who are addicts living on the street or wherever they can. I pray a lot more for them and their families. I wonder if they have people worried. I wonder if they know that someone somewhere is thinking about them and worrying about them every day. I wonder if they know that their heavenly Father loves them and wants them to have a better life than what they have chosen for themselves. I wonder if you know that . . . I think you do. I know that you know God and His love. I saw it in your face when you were at rehab. I saw the love you felt for Him. I know that is still inside you. I know those seeds were planted.

It's hard to be patient and wait for God's timing. But I guess that is my part in this. Wait and pray. God's will not mine.

JANUARY 8, 2017

So my prayer as I close this letter, I pray you feel God's love today and every day... even if only for a moment. I pray your eyes are opened to the life you are choosing and the fact that you can change it. I pray you know I love you.

Goodnight, sweet girl.

Mom

# January 22, 2017

I finally heard from you today. Got a picture on Snapchat. You look good. Your eyes aren't right, but I guess I'm used to that by now. You're alive. That's my focus. You're alive.

Things here are good. I'm working. Christian and Pheobe are going to school. Your brother is working graveyard shifts at Walmart, so I don't see him a lot. He sleeps most days. Life is going on. I don't know what that means, but it is going. We are all taking baby steps to keep moving forward. Your dad is staying busy with work. He keeps looking at me waiting for me to fall apart, but I'm not. I'm really OK. We have been going to church on a regular basis, and I feel the difference it is making inside me. I don't cry all the time during worship anymore. Only certain songs make me cry . . . and it isn't always from sadness. Sometimes, I cry with joy because I know that God will bring you home someday. I know it. I do miss you. All the time. But I stay busy and focused on those around me.

I try to spend more time with Tanner. He still has some anger, but he seems to be OK. Like me, he's staying busy. Christian and Pheobe are doing good. They moved in, and it kind of feels like they have always been here, at least for me it feels that way. They have been around us since birth, so there are no awkward moments of getting to know about us.

My real struggle now is in the quiet moments. At night when your dad has already fallen asleep . . . when no one is up and moving around . . . when the house is quiet except for the night noises, that's when my brain runs rampant. I always picture the worst. It's almost always an overdose. Sometimes, the cops knock and tell me; sometimes, it's a phone call. You are always alone. I think that is what haunts me the most. To picture you alone and afraid. I always take it to God . . . you know after I have lain there for an hour crying . . . but eventually, I pray. And a calm comes over me. A calm that is better than anything I can get from medicine. A calm that I cannot explain. He whispers promises of safety. I hear verses in my head and usually a song. I almost always fall asleep to a song.

God is so good.

Always,

# February 11, 2017

Lilly,

Today we had Julanie's baby shower, and you came. I had spoken with you about it, but never really thought you would come. To be honest I wasn't even sure you were still close by. Anyway, the shower was good. Lots of family and friends. Lots of presents and laughs. It was almost a good day. I was busy the whole time since I was sort of the hostess.

You and I didn't get a chance to talk. Just a few hugs here and there. You look OK. Not great. Still too skinny. Too much makeup. It's so dark when you're using . . . like you're trying to hide the person you were. I don't know. I read too many books. I always try to make everything have some deep meaning. You're probably just putting makeup on so dark because you like it that way. I always think too much about every little detail when it comes to you.

It was a good day until I heard you start telling people goodbye. You had walked into the living room earlier and sat down next to me and gave me a hard hug. I knew the goodbye was coming. I couldn't face you. I ran and hid in the bathroom. I heard you leave, and I just fell to the floor and tried to cry silently so that no one would hear. Someone did. Carla, Pheobe, and Christian's mom came in. She tried to hug me, and I pushed her away. How could she hug me for being heartbroken about my daughter using meth when she was doing the same thing! I know that my anger was misplaced, but in that moment, I just wanted her to leave me alone. I will say, God sent the right person. I stopped crying. Turned off my feelings and walked out of the bathroom; I went out and acted like I was perfectly fine. Everyone stayed and talked and laughed. I pretended. They all left. I cleaned.

I went to bed that night and cried silently, so I wouldn't wake your dad. I am almost a pro at crying with no sound. If I could just find a way to make my nose quit running. I finally decided to go ahead and write another letter. If anything, it helps me get my feelings out. I can't really talk to anyone. Well, that's not true. I could. I just feel like at this point people are tired of hearing me. I am tired of hearing me.

Anyway, I'm glad you came, and I got to see you. I love you so very much. I miss you.

Always,
Mom

# February 20, 2017

Today, I am stalking you on Facebook. I haven't heard from you since the shower. I mean you send a picture every few days or so, but just like a proof of life picture. You know I'm crazy with worry so even in your drug-induced stupor, you remember to let me know you're alive. I'm sure God plays a part in that as well. I am a slow learner, but I am learning. I really do worry less. I'm sure you won't believe that, but I do. Writing these letters helps. I guess it's a kind of therapy to pretend like I'm telling you all the things I would say if you were here. Sometimes, I can even make it through a whole hour without worrying at all. Sometimes. Anyway, I am looking at your Facebook page where you posted a beautiful picture of yourself. You're lying on a bed, and you used a filter that gave you a crown of flowers. You're wearing a bandana print tank top; the picture is black and white. It takes my breath away for a minute.

I hope you are OK. The fact that you are such a beautiful girl scares me even more. There is so much evil in this world—evil that would use that beauty for terrible things.

I am still praying. Every day. All the time.

# February 22, 2017

Today, I walked into my classroom and on my desk lay a beautiful necklace with a wing and a Bible verse: *He shall cover you with His feathers, and under His wings you shall take refuge; His truth shall be your shield and buckler"* (Psalm 91:4).

Whoever left the necklace wrote the Bible verse on a sticky note. I am overwhelmed with peace and love from this small gesture. I found out later that Stephanie left it for me—the same Stephanie who told us about Teen Challenge. She truly has been a godsend. As terrible as this whole chapter has been, it has brought about so many blessings that I might not have noticed otherwise. God really does shine the most in the hard times. I want to sit and cry, but who has time for that?

I wanted to write and tell you that someday when you look back at this season of your life and you feel guilt, please don't. We love you. We would go through this over again and still love you. I am learning unconditional love. I feel my heart opening up in areas of my life that had been closed for a long time. I'm discovering love for a mom who left and chose drugs; love for a dad who was there eventually but just barely; love for a grandmother who tried the best she could; love for a brother who chose a bad path; and love for uncles, aunts, and even strangers who have been lost in this life of addiction. I see them in a different light now.

I love you, daughter. Always,
Mom

# March 20, 2017

I don't even have words to describe the joy I felt this evening. All my kids were home. ALL. You and Steven came to have dinner with the rest of us. My heart is beyond happy. I guess it was the end of February when you called and said that you and Steven had a date. Since then, you have moved in with him.

You call me every other day and let me know what is going on. You are you. I am not sure how it all happened, but I don't care. You guys look happy. You look healthy. This month has been a whirlwind of activity for you. I am still waiting . . . watching to see if I am wrong, but I really think this might be the end of this chapter in hell and the beginning of a new chapter. One with more happy stories. Tonight was great. We all sat and talked and ate, and of course, I took pictures. I don't remember talking to anyone too much. I just watched in awe. You and Tanner and Christian and Pheobe and Steven. It was such a beautiful, answered prayer for me. I am not sure what will happen after this, but I know this night will forever be one of my favorite memories.

When I was growing up feeling so alone, the thing I wanted most in the world was a family. A big family. Tonight, we didn't have enough chairs at the table. How silly for that to make me happy, but it did. I understand why God waits for us to choose Him. It is amazing to see everyone here because this is where they choose to be. I am hoping this feeling stays in my heart for a while. I won't lie and say I am expecting everything to be perfect from here on out, but it really feels like this is a turn.

# January 17, 2019

I haven't written any letters in quite some time. I stopped writing because you started calling me almost every day. You and Steven have been doing well. Next month, you will have been clean for two years. The first few months were hard. I kept watching and waiting. I know that isn't what I was supposed to do, but it's hard to let go of fear. I prayed a lot. God is always there. I kept thinking you wouldn't be able to do it living in Artesia around the same people. Next thing I knew, you guys were moving to Roswell with Steven's mom.

That was OK for a little while, but she started making bad decisions, and again my fear rose, but you guys went to his nana. She had a place in Ruidoso, and you guys moved there. You both got jobs. You got a dog. You started living life. Without drugs. I went up every couple of weeks to see you. Dad went several times also. It was amazing to watch you growing into a life we had prayed for. I had another scare when the Ruidoso's plan fell apart, and you guys moved home with us. You were doing OK, but you got pregnant. That was great; we were all so excited. Then a couple of months in, you started bleeding and cramping. You miscarried. I was afraid that would push you over the edge. It didn't. Steven helped you through it. I was so blessed to watch you both grow into adults. In March, you and Steven and Christian got baptized at church. I could see God working in all your lives. It was beautifully amazing to me.

In April, you guys got married. Nothing big. Just the courthouse. You were so happy. Yesterday, you gave birth to a son. He was little at five pounds, nine ounces, but he is perfect. You were glowing as you held him. I was there for the delivery—the delivery of my first grandchild. Yes. I am blessed. I know how this story could have played out. So many addicts never break free. So many overdose. So many pretty girls disappear. I know how it could have played out because I watched it happen in my nightmares night after night. Tonight, I sit and watch you hold your son. I see your husband look at you and smile. I know that God loves you even more than I do. I don't know what happens after this. I do know that no matter where you are in life, the best thing I can do in every situation is to pray and give it to God. If that is the only thing that I learned through all this, I am so very blessed. I know that praying and trusting God is the reason I made it through this storm. He always sent exactly what I needed—a song, a bird, a phone call from a friend, a smile from my husband, and sometimes the harsh words I needed to hear. Always exactly what I needed when I needed it. What an awesome God I serve.

What an amazing Father I have. If you ever read these letters, please know that your hard story will be used to help so many. You will use it as your testimony. I will use it as part of mine. Don't ever feel guilt or shame. You, my daughter, are a warrior. The devil tried to trick you and steal away your life, but God used it for good. And now my cup runs over.

God is good **all** the time.

www.ingramcontent.com/pod-product-compliance
Lightning Source LLC
LaVergne TN
LVHW051525070426
835507LV00023B/3316